# Slowly, I Grow

## John Doriot

# Slowly, I Grow

## Other books by John Doriot:

Novels:
Litter
The Cures

Short Story Collections:
Intersections
Crossroads
Grimmer Folk Stories
Idioms

Poetry:
Irritable Vowels
From Sorrow to Tomorrow

Children's Books:
Doozy
Oh, Where'd You Go, Oreo?
A Dog I Know Called Oreo
What Would Oreo Say, If She Could Talk Today?

## Author's websites:

https://oreodoriotbooks.com

https://minddriftbooks.com

## Dedication

*for all my ghosts*

# Author's Note

This book is the culmination of three years of thoughts, ideas, and emotions. Love, Beauty, Grief, Solace, Prayer, Healing, Awe, Anger, Anxiety, Despair, Depression, Hope, and Faith are all words that could be used to describe the mood of these poems. Questions about myself, the world, or why bad things happen to good people, were frequently asked as I explored different ways to convey my feelings or thoughts. These moments of reflection often took place in nature as I find refuge in its beauty and its ability to allow my mind to find its spiritual roots. I see God within nature and it has been amazing to understand how this evolution has taken place over the years.

I have believed in a higher power for a long time and always felt closer to God within nature, but a spark was lit when I saw how God intervened when my dog was badly hurt several years ago. Through our walks together, I was able to commune with Him and watch Him heal her and me simultaneously. My awareness of the beautiful world around me changed. Going forward, when I spend time in nature each day, I find myself not only communing with God but also, seeing and hearing what I ignored in the past while exploring my emotions and ideas. As I was gathering these poems into a book, I was unsure how to group them at first. Reading them over and over, general themes began to emerge, and thus, "Joy," "I Wonder," "Unexplained," and "Bliss" became the chapter titles.

The poems under the heading of "Joy" are reflective of those times when I feel good physically and mentally. The day is beyond beautiful. There is jubilation created from the news a procedure went well for a friend or a family member, or their illness was cured. Perhaps, someone I love achieves success or I watch my granddaughter smile, giggle, or do something for the first time. All seems right with the world.

The "I Wonder" chapter contains poems expressing mixed feelings: sorrow, happiness, grief, and solace. The poems may have some negative aspects, but they still convey hope and a desire for a better outcome.

"Unexplained" poems are those thoughts and questions that bother me because I cannot find an answer for them within myself, and I do not understand why we can be such thoughtless and cruel creatures to one another. I frequently fall back on the teachings of C. S. Lewis in many of these situations. I find his writings to be very helpful in coping with the knowledge, regardless of how much we want utopia in the world, we will never find it here. That is not to say we should give up doing everything we can to make the world a better place because, when we can, we must help those who need our help. And in that regard, we also need to help ourselves each day by just sitting back and recognizing all the amazing things the world has to offer. I have said this before. God doesn't make a bad day, but you have to want to find the beauty around you, and I certainly understand how doing so isn't always easy to achieve. I still struggle with this periodically and when I do, I seek refuge in the woods and in the world where I can write.

The final set of poems falls under the heading of "Bliss" and was generated by the birth of my granddaughter, Joan Alyce Doriot. For those of you who have grandchildren, no further explanation is needed. For those who do not have grandchildren, I can tell you, they are indeed a gift from heaven.

If you read my other fictional work, you will find I always place personal aspects of my life within the stories or books. These personal elements may take the form of street names, cities, towns, and locations I have lived in, been to, or stayed for a night or two. Some of the events in those fictional stories are inspired by things that happened to me. I have not personally seen any ghosts or monsters in my closet, attic, basement, or under my bed, but in my recent book "Idioms," one of the stories is based on an event that truly did happen to me, along with some ghostly embellishment. The idea for the book "Litter," was sparked by an incident that happened in my work environment, while some of the unique and quirky aspects of the story's characters came from people I met. And those ghosts and monsters or victims in my books may have the name of a friend, or someone, well, let's just say, who was not a friend, and leave it at that. I get a kick out of doing so and my friends do too.

But the overriding themes of my poetry are not fictional and are very personal. These are the thoughts, ideas, and feelings that I have and continue to have. The questions I ask are ones I have asked and continue to ask. Poetry is a journey I will be on for as long as I can walk and form words. I hope you will find my journey reflects your journey at some point in your life. I have read these poems many times, and the words continue to resonate with me. I hope you will connect to them and come back to your favorites whenever you feel the reason to do so. I believe we share much more in common than we think.

Lastly, I wish to say a few words about the title. It comes from a poem in the book, titled, "Slowly, I Go." When you read it, I believe you will immediately think I am writing about either birth or death; but actually, I am exploring the fact that the beginning and end of life share a common theme – pain, which I believe, constantly tests our faith. I know it does mine. We cannot help but see the suffering that takes place throughout the world and wonder how God can allow such terrible things to happen. We have moments in our lives when we question where God is because of the mental, physical, and spiritual pain we feel. Every day, I ask God to help me to become a better version of myself. Some days I succeed. Some days I fail, but I can say, I will never forsake my faith. It would indeed be a bleak world without it.

# Acknowledgments

Thanks to my wife Jeanne, my patient consultant, sounding board, and editor who is a rock I rely upon on a daily basis.

Thank you to my son Alex for his cover design work, edits, and constant support, and thanks to my granddaughter Joan for reminding me what angels look like on Earth.

Thanks to my faithful companion Oreo. If empathy had four paws, I am certain it would look like her.

And special thanks to Peggy Mercer, my editor for this book. Your input and guidance enabled me to grow as a writer and helped my poetry blossom. For more information - https://peggymercerworldwide.org

# Table of Contents

## Joy

Good Friday --- 2
Spring Walk --- 3
A day in May --- 4
Prom Day --- 5
A walk after rain --- 6
Green --- 7
Work --- 8
Circles --- 11
Tunnel Vision --- 12
Slowly, I Go ---13
Reach --- 14
Early summer morning after the rain --- 15
Gold --- 16
43 --- 17
Summer being summer --- 18
A spring in her step --- 19
Awake --- 20
Both eyes --- 21
Best Friend --- 22
The Pound --- 23
Black and White Overalls --- 24
I Refuse to Give Up --- 25
Ethereal --- 26
The muted forest --- 27
mushrooms --- 28
Hopeful --- 29
One of the last days of summer --- 30
The Beginning of Fall --- 31
The Owl --- 32
The weary traveler --- 33
The First Day in October --- 34

A fall walk --- 35
Wonderfall --- 36
An early day in November --- 37
seconds --- 38
One Year Later --- 39
December One --- 40
Paperwhites --- 41
Today Sang --- 42
O Holy Night is Sometimes Not Sung in Church --- 43
Kindred Spirits --- 44
Learning to read --- 45
Although --- 46
Skyblue --- 47
Spring Trees --- 48
A day at the end of March in Charleston, Tennessee --- 49
Antiques --- 50
ode --- 51
Something to consider --- 52
Daylight Savings Time --- 53
A beautiful mind --- 54

# I Wonder

Fissures --- 59
Trees --- 61
Dead Trees --- 62
A Wooded Path --- 63
promises --- 64
A beautiful picture of winter --- 65
Winter walk --- 66
A Winter Storm on the Horizon --- 67
respite --- 68
A Lifetime --- 69
A moment in time --- 71
An old empty pickle jar --- 73

The Lamp --- 74
Silent Night --- 75
Outer Space --- 76
It's not easy to understand --- 77
Brown eyes --- 78
Behavioral Observation --- 79
Storms --- 80
Suppose --- 81
Reading Glasses --- 82
Confinement --- 83
Reflections --- 84
A summer day --- 85
A Prayer --- 87
Moss --- 88
Shadow land --- 89
A hot summer day ---90
The First Day of September --- 91
There in the air somewhere --- 93
one --- 94
Working in the garden and woods is good for the soil --- 95
A recent airport visit --- 96
Van Buren Arkansas --- 97
600 more miles on a 2500 mile trip completed in 4 days --- 98
Solitary --- 99
Rainy day walk --- 102
Some things never get old --- 103
Shoveling dirt --- 104
Waves --- 105
Joy ---- 106
Changing of the Guard --- 108
Reunion --- 109
Fifty-one weeks ago --- 110
Solace --- 111
A Fall Prayer --- 112
Not long ago --- 113

I will miss him --- 114
little is better than none and more is better than little --- 115
Ghosts --- 116
Wisps --- 118
The next morning when most people are at work --- 119

# Unexplained

mud --- 121
Daisies --- 122
Lofty Dreams --- 123
Monterey Bay --- 124
Variation --- 125
What next --- 126
The sky was dark and gray before the sun came out --- 127
Sadness in the air --- 128
Pray --- 129
Connections --- 130
A funny looking Owl --- 131

# Bliss

Hand me downs --- 133
First Time ---134
Sigh --- 135
Wish --- 136
Floating on a Cloud ---138
Moment --- 139
A Walk in the Woods --- 140
One Day --- 142
Words --- 143
The Eating Suit --- 145
One going on two --- 146

# Joy

"No soul that seriously and constantly desires joy will ever miss it. Those who seek find. To those who knock it is opened."

C. S. Lewis

## Good Friday

The woods are an ocean of
green in early spring.
The trees are tall
wooden masts
atop wooden ships
floating beneath
the morning star.
I smile as they sail
somewhere near,
somewhere far.
If I am marooned
on this island for the
rest of my life,
I will not ask for rescue,
because I am already saved.

## Spring Walk

The sky is baby blue
and cotton white
filling in
the space of
a green puzzle
of treetops.
Chirps and tweets
and other bird speak,
echo from the sides
of the road.
A teal hummingbird
hovers over
emerald, rust tipped
holly bushes.
They remind me
of Fairies or Sprites
and I smile
like a child
reading about
magical woodland
beings
for the first time.

## A day in May

The small and GIANT tent-peg
trees of willow oak and pine
anchor just fine,
the green revival canopy
            extending
      over the asphalt road.
Holes in the tent cover
reflect
Celestial Bodies
creating a mosaic
of sh a dows
on the gr ay and sil ver
can vas wel com ing
painted feet.
A magical and spiritual show
            changing
every
day
has started.
Though tickets are free,
It requires
audience participation.

## Prom Day

The days are full
of youthful energy.
Magnolia is in her
emerald green dress
with a creamy
white corsage and
ready for the prom picture.
The photo will be
placed and organized
into an album
and forgotten
and then remembered
at first with fondness,
and then with a yearning
for steady limbs from a
    family tree of
    weathered
     wisdom.

## A walk after rain

A spring rain has come and gone.
There is a green sheen on the
abundant leaves hanging down
from tiny fingers and strong limbs.
Trees talk to each other
as rain drops from one leaf to another.
Light from a cloudless and sunless sky
is fluorescent and profuse.
I lose myself in the picture
only to be awakened
by orange and yellow Daylilies
nodding hello,
glowing for too short a time.
Thankfully,
there will be many more greetings
from the buds filling up with radiance.

## Green

The woods are green,
dark green, pale green, light green, yellow green,
forest green, fern green, pine green, grass green, clover
green, moss green.
Where is the color in green?
I once asked this question on a thousand walks,
unaware of the nuance of nature.
But slowly, I grow and am green for the next journey.

## Work

To live a life that has no
work, does not resonate as
a life well lived.
Life is work; work
that provides pleasure
only you sometimes
celebrate.
Work is family and
life itself.
Synonyms.
Work is pain, esteem,
pride, sorrow, Joy,
Love and Beauty.
I sing a song not
everyone hears but
it does not matter,
because I hear it
even when I cannot hear
anything else.
My prayers are work
and are heard
beyond stained glass.
They are just as welcome
amidst tall green stalks
of corn, or among many
rows of tomatoes,
lettuce or butterbeans.
Work is wood
reflecting the ageless
face of nature
smiling.

The lines connect the
past and the present
and are magnificently
flawed.
It is holy.
Work is children,
And grandchildren,
And great-grandchildren,
And friends,
And sisters,
And brothers,
And cousins,
And coworkers,
Who cast a long shadow
onto my own,
that is present
still today
in sun and shade.
Work is a marriage
that seems like
it happened yesterday
until you add up
all the yesterdays.
I find solace in the hills
and valleys and
Mountains and streams,
and in cut grass,
or tilled soil
I see or smell
along the many roads
I travel
and upon the land
which I share for a
Moment in time.

A humble spirit
welcomes
Nature and work.
I work because I can
and its value is not
always measured by
man's clock.
Work is selfless and
I am Always
Grateful when I
Am at work.


*(For my father-in-law, an amazing man)*

## Circles

At one point in time,
You say
"I remember when" or
"When I was growing up."
And at that point in time,
You remember.
You remember your
Grandparents saying the
Exact words.
And at that point in time,
You remember.
You remember your
Parents saying the
Exact words.
And at that point in time,
Smile.
It is a good point in time.

## Tunnel Vision

My dog and I walk
through a green tunnel
of tree limbs today.
The trees celebrate
this time of green with
full branches for many guests

      that

Flitter and twitter,
Leap and peep,
Crawl and call,
Fly and cry,
Lurch and chirp,
Scatter and chatter,

      and

Climb and find
shelter and food
atop and along,
in silence and song,
beneath and between,
seen and unseen,
in the abundance of trees.
The tree shades are shadows
we do not fear but welcome.
Birds encircle us with surround sound
as we walk along the road.
Our sight, mine and Oreo's,
is no longer sharp,

but our vision
      at
this time of the day,
      at
this moment in time,

Is one of extreme clarity.

## Slowly, I Go

Slowly, I go
Slowly, I flow
Over stone.

Slowly, I go
Slowly, I know
All Alone.

Slowly, I go
Slowly, wind blows
Away bone.

Slowly, all hurt
Ground into dirt
And I moan.

Slowly, I grow
Into a soul
And I'm home.

**Reach**

When I come home, her alone-looking eyes
go away and she stays by my side
If I sit or walk or go anywhere, she wants to be there
How lucky can someone be to have another being see only
the best in you when you are far from being the best in you
They call her a rescue dog, unaware the term has dual
meaning

## Early summer morning after the rain

The sunbeams streaming through the trees this morning
appear to have form,
distinct shafts of light with various shades of intensity.
A man of faith would call them evidence of the divine.
There was a heavy rain last night and science would suggest
sunbeams are always there but only seen when viewed
through an opening against an opaque background like trees.
The particles of dust and steam make a gleam, stirred up by
the heat of the sun and animals on the run.
It looks to me without a doubt like a mystical bridge of light
for the woodland sprites to move about.

I accept all explanations willingly.

## Gold

Golden leaves fall to the ground sometimes, as a single drop of sun.

Sometimes as a bushel of golden delicious apples tipped over from the top of the tree falling to the ground with crumpled sounds.

Sometimes like thin strips of golden delicious apples hanging onto the tree for a moment before they let go and float in the air full of light,

hovering over the ground until they find a spot to light.

Sometimes they jump from the ground and move elsewhere as if a spirit is moving them to a better spot to winter.

Perhaps a spirit moves all of them balancing atop a golden leaf with a brown spine moving up and down on buoyant waves of wind.

All I know is I am a rich man with all this gold to spend.

## 43

I'm flying across the United States
but my heart is in another place.
It lingers at home
with Oreo and little Joan.
But there is something I wish to say,
tomorrow is a special day.
43 years ago I found a friend
who wanted to be there at the end,
and now we're headed down Highway One
along the road the Pacific runs.
To celebrate again with something new;
to celebrate again an ocean view.
To continue the journey I began,
43 years ago with a friend.

*(This was written for my wife. We did indeed make this trip, but it didn't turn out the way we planned. She got covid while traveling and we didn't want to risk infecting others by flying home. Since I was still negative, I loaded up the car and we headed home. This trip home was a nightmare, but I knew I would eventually get sick if we didn't go ahead and leave and who knows how long we would have been stuck on the west coast in a dark motel room. Once again, God was looking out for us. I was able to keep her isolated from others, and she was able to get medicine and could rest while I drove as long as I could each day. I didn't get sick until about an hour away from home. It was a trip we will never forget and even though we will always include the horrible journey home in our memories, we will never forget the beauty of the Oregon coastline. I hope to return there with her one day and maybe we can take a little girl named Joan with us! It is indeed a magical place full of mountains on one side of the road, with the Pacific Ocean, beach, and mountains on the beach on the other, and even mountains in the ocean. Truly spectacular.)*

## Summer being summer

The crepe myrtles continue to bloom though their shows are
sold out and they are packing up to move on
It is humid this morning when my dog and I walk but that's
summer being summer

It's warm and green though some tree's leaves begin to fall as
if they heard an early call to change clothes
It's August and the hours are slow and easy,
but soon will come days, much more breezy

I can wait for those winds to blow, you know?
For I have learned to not let today get away
As I enjoy the days of now I have found
with summer being summer.

## A spring in her step

My dog Oreo, this morning trots down the road with more assurance than she's had in a long time.

It is summer but she has a spring in her step.

The sun changes the color of trees into lighter shades of green and all of the trees are full and many extend a limb toward a relative or a stranger across the road.

My dog is curious and stops at many places and walks into wooded areas she has never been.

She even let a crow know these are her woods today and to fly away as she lunged at it as it moved from tree to tree until it could see it needed to leave.

My dog looks back at me as if to say I could fly if given a chance and I smiled because I saw her do so when given the chance.

## Awake

I cannot believe what I took for granted less than six months
ago
Every morning I walk with my dog down our wooded street
and regardless of the season there is beauty
Today is no exception
Trees are wet from the evening before and all are vibrant
colors of green
The end of the street has a misty steeple arising from the
trees like a scene from a movie or a church in the distance
The weather is pleasant and after our walk, I work in the
garden planting golden sedum, more green than gold and
creeping jenny, more gold than green, along the new
walkway of various tones of brown flagstones
The garden is taking shape and I enjoy working in it every
day
I believe creeping jenny has the ability to spread through
more than one kind of soil.

## Both eyes

In my dog's eyes
I see God's eyes.
Unconditional love.
Eternal love.
Forgiving love.

In the bluest skies,
I see God's eyes.
Unconditional love.
Eternal love.
Forgiving love.

And on the day I die,
I hope I see, both sets of eyes.


*(Dedicated to Cindy, Maggie, and Oreo)*

## Best Friend

I feel her heart beating against my leg.
This gentle soul is less than genteel when she sleeps.
She growls without malice, her body twitches,
Her legs and feet pedal as she races through her dreams!
I sit here wide awake and look down at her
and try to imagine how the muted color palette
in her dreams reflects such a beautiful world.


*(For Oreo)*

## The Pound

The pound is a breeding ground for aristocracy for pets as fine as democracy. I think our constitution with much elocution would say these furry companions and their plights are endowed with unalienable rights and among those rights are the following:

To love and be loved
To greet people like they are your best friend every time you see them
To be happy and play in grass and mud and water and snow
To sleep whenever possible and as much as needed
To enjoy their food every time and never go hungry
To crawl into someone's lap and stay there as long as they want
To be in the moment for the sake of being in the moment
To not worry about the past or the future
To provide comfort to friends when they sense it is needed
To treasure life

I think God visits the pound often and provides comfort and hope. I think He would like it if we visited there more often and provided comfort and hope for pets to cope with loneliness while they wait for a home.

## Black and White Overalls

The supply store
suggested
Tractors.

The time of year
suggested
Prayers.

The newspaper ad
suggested
Abandoned.

Her name
suggested
Family.

Throw up in the car
suggested
Fear.

Her own pillow
suggested
Shadow.

The way she settled
suggested
Zuzu's petals.

*(This poem is about the day I found Oreo. She was a rescue pet at the Tractor Supply Store. We were told by the rescue agency she often threw up when traveling in the car. She did for several weeks but that went away when she knew we wouldn't. The last stanza refers to one of my favorite movies, "It's a Wonderful Life," because Oreo has certainly made it one.)*

## I Refuse to Give Up

Cancer killed my mother,
My father and my brother.
It also had a hand,
In killing my best friend.

My sisters and my wife,
Cancer attacked their life,
And my Cousin and
Father and Brother-in-law.
But survivors, they are all.

Even at my door, it asked to come in,
And then attacked more friends.
It seems the story never ends
Until you find a way to win
With Hope.

It's the only way we cope,
Because every day we Hope.

*"Miracles are a retelling in small letters of the very same story which is written across the whole world in letters too large for some of us to see." - C. S. Lewis*

## Ethereal

In autumn, nature writes a book.
You leaf through the pages and are
amazed at the colorful language.
You realize some of the vibrant pages
don't make a sound when you turn them
while others crackle when you touch them
and you know it's an old book read a million times,
but the story is as fresh as the day it was written.
When you read about the large black and brown dogs,
barks leap from the pages
but you don't feel scared, just aware.
You read what is forevergreen and it engulfs the character and
makes you take deep breaths, or cry, or laugh, or shout, before
you close your eyes and rest.

## The muted forest

The muted forest is silent providing solace
Nature's jigsaw puzzle pieces lay at my feet no longer vibrant
but distinct
Why does grief open your eyes to the beauty of the world when
the beauty of the world should blind you?
The red bird stares at me with mercy before it flies away
As it starts to rain, I pull the hood of my jacket over my head
and continue to walk
Alone but unafraid, knowing the muted forest will once again
speak to me with a radiant voice.

## mushrooms

fluorescent orange mushrooms light up the woods

oyster shell white mushrooms can no longer hide beneath the ground

washed away from the rains yesterday

brown jellyfish shaped mushrooms sit on the forest floor until it rains some more

the woods today are oceans away from the coast

but they too boast about their own vibrant inhabitants

## Hopeful

I watched a little bird fall from the nest.
I wasn't sure if it would die or survive
so I provided care until it flew into the air and left.
I hoped for the best for what happened next
Because flying is what birds do best!

## One of the last days of summer

I see dark wet leaves on green grass this morning.
The cool breeze suggests a long sleeve shirt
will soon be welcome.
Summer won't last much longer
but robins still forage in the yard, hurrying.
The trees in the woods are still green
but there's a spot of rust here and there
suggesting change corrodes the air.
The dogwood on my rocky bank
makes me think of fall
with some leaves the color of a peach just out of reach.
Next to the creek, a saucer size mushroom emerges
out of dirt and shade and appears crafted
from beautiful brown leather.
I wonder if it will last more than a day or fade away,
after showing me the essence of its presence.
But even when it is gone, I am sure I will see all nature of
shades and textures as I walk along the wooded path
on one of the last days of the summer.

## The Beginning of Fall

I never tire of watching green leaves burst
into figurative flames of red, orange, and yellow
as fall begins to call.
It is a lyrical voice loud and vibrant
providing crowds excitement,
and my dog and I,
a colorful sky of fireworks.

## The Owl

We shared the country roads with an owl
and somehow found our way
through cloudy mists of gray and white
and reflective views of yellow light
as we continued throughout the night.
Thankfully, arrival was met with survival
and when we stopped to rest
the owl moved on, further west.
In Tennessee, the rooster crowed as the sun rose
and with dawn, life moved on.
I thanked the owl for showing the way;
as a new day, lifted dark away
from all around us,
revealing so much promise.


*(This poem grew out of a trip we had to take in the middle of the night after learning my wife's father had a pulmonary embolism. Neither my wife nor I see that well to drive in the dark but that night I had no trouble at all seeing. Again, God intervened on our travels and with her father. If you showed his CT scan to any doctor, they would shake their head and say, "How is this man still alive?" Not only is the man alive, he just celebrated another year of life. 92 years young. I didn't see an owl though, that is just a metaphor for night.)*

## The weary traveler

The weary traveler sat down on the sofa and sighed.
The sigh reflected relief, gratitude and awe, considering all he saw.
He had seen and done things he had never done before and right now, he doubted he could do one thing more.
He wondered about time and age as he moved from the sofa to his favorite recliner.
He lay back, closed his eyes and rested.
From across the room, he looked like a Norman Rockwell painting of an old man at peace and asleep in his favorite chair, in a familiar corner of the house he had made a home.
Even though life changes everyone, it appeared as if it had collapsed upon his shoulders all at once with an overwhelming weight, and I felt a sadness overcome me.
Philosophy and Theology intertwined in my mind as I remembered all of the wonderful occasions with him as stories filled the air of family get-togethers;
And then I saw him look at me and his eyes sparkled, and within them, I saw many more miles of new journeys.


*(My father-in-law had less than a 1% chance of survival. He had a "saddle" pulmonary embolus. Three days after being in ICU, he was at home. Two days later, I was walking with him down the street in front of his house with his oxygen cylinder wrapped around his shoulder. Four weeks later, he walked a mile with his oxygen. Six weeks later, he no longer required oxygen and was back to a normal routine, which meant working in the garden all morning and in his workshop in the afternoon, after lunch and a nap. He continues to do that every day.)*

## The First Day in October

After a cloudless day, dark and gray,
blue sky and light, emerged from rainy night.
Patches of light became gaps within woods
and tiny spotlights atop the wooded floor.
Yellow and gold and green and brown
filled the ground as trees shed their leaves.
A brown hawk grabbed a limb
as I stood there and stared at him
until he saw a need to fly
his rhythmic wings, a silent bye
and on this day October 1,
I think our fall has begun.

## A fall walk

A squadron of geese honked and flew by
as I happened to stop and look to the sky
Squirrels chattered as it mattered
when Oreo walked by
Yellow and brown colored the trees
but one full of orange, was a flare to see
A blanket of leaves covered the ground
as more and more fell and fluttered around.
The air was crisp as a brittle leaf
crushed by Oreo sniffing around
The chirps and the tweets
kept time with our feet
for the seasons have changed;
a welcome exchange
when Oreo and I talked
on a fall walk.

## Wonderfall

A puzzle of color lies on the wooded ground
no longer just brown.
Orange and yellow and red are in bed
with apricot and maroon this afternoon.
There are islands of green winter grasses
in clumps and masses,
and the trees are beginning to paint the woods
with colors that ensure
each day, changes what the eyes see.
What a wonderful day to be.
Indeed, we've walked into a Wonderfall.

## An early day in November

Wrinkled and crinkled hands and pine needle fingers cover
the face of the wooded floor
It is November and the trees begin to bare their souls to those
who care to listen
Limbs are twisted toward the silver blue sky and out toward
their neighbors in all different directions
with shapes and curves and angles suggesting geometry is an
infinite art form
The wind rustles through the leaves and the trees wave to me
in unison and when they do,
I see patches of green and brown and yellow and rust and
peach lingering for a little while longer,
which prompts me to do the same.

## seconds

The storm made its presence known before it retreated back home into clouds,
but there is another storm on the horizon.
Yet now, there are seconds before the next storm is present,
so my dog and I walk through the woods.
Oh what beauty in the cold air of woods, now bare!
There are picturesque moments everywhere!
Ones, I would not have seen a year ago, a fact not lost within my thoughts.
As I walk along the wooded road, I realize here, time is not measured by man but by nature itself.
It cannot be confined by its boundaries.
Yes, time is truth, but with numerous windows as we blink our eyes and glimpse the infinite.

## One Year Later

The day is a cloudy shade
from storms made
on the horizon.
The hills of Tennessee are not a threat to us,
unlike last year,
when we felt the flash and gash and fury.
Today, the sun breaks through the gray
and though the day for giving thanks is over,
It never ever goes away.

*(This poem reflects one year later after my dog and wife were attacked and I almost lost Oreo. Thankfully, Jeanne was not hurt badly but Oreo suffered grave injuries. The elderly gentleman who owned the attacking dog fell down over Oreo to protect her, sustaining multiple bites from his own dog. If he had not done so, Oreo would not be alive today. I will never forget the act of sacrifice and kindness.)*

## December One

December one told a cold story.
The air was still, yet there was a cold chill
wrapped around my face like a scarf.
The weather and woods suggested winter.
An angelic cloud in the fluorescent blue sky offered hope.
Another walk with my dog prompted joy
beneath the glint of sun
on cold, but warm, December One.

## Paperwhites

Paperwhites in winter light, are a sight to see

Winter white, is so bright, beneath the unleafed trees

A winter bloom, not too soon, to raise up all our hopes

A winter flower, gives us room, to keep our dreams afloat

In the skies of white and blue, and through the trees so bare

There is no hindrance to restrain, all our love and prayers

A paperwhite, so simple yet

It helps me not forget.

## Today Sang

Today was cold and reminded me of a year ago
when Oreo cried and our eyes filled with tears and
We feared the worst.
But the worst was simply a fear
and though the road to recovery was long
We stayed on it and I prayed on it every day
and we walked the wooded path
a little more each day
until I could say at last
the wind was our friend again.
Although the woods are silent today,
the noise of footsteps and pawsteps
Sing beneath the arms of the sun.

## O Holy Night is Sometimes Not Sung in Church

The temperature is seventeen and the wind is mean.
It feels like one degree for my little dog and me,
as we venture outside with her by my side.
It is indeed too cold for a walk
but I am not sure my dog of black and white
will see another silent night
considering the storm she endured last year.
So we walk and share
one more Christmas Eve together,
Beautiful, in any kind of weather.

## Kindred Spirits

The old dog stopped, turned around, and waited.
Waited for the old man to catch up,
As if to say "come on, come on, we're waiting."
But it's okay today, especially today.
They were kindred spirits on a Christmas morning.
And felt no need to hurry
Or worry with the cold,
Just because they were old.
Within the embrace of the Sun
The walk was a glorious one,
And I will remember it forever.

## Learning to read

The trees write in cursive in winter
and I love the elegant words I see
as I learn to read.
I think it will be a while
and many miles of this stylish look,
before I finish, this wondrous book.

## Although

Although there was no sun,
the trees in the woods cast long shadows.
Although the thermometer suggested a jacket,
it did not feel cold.
Although the woods were silent and somber
the little black and white dog walking beside me
enabled me to see through the clouds
and I did not wonder how.

## Skyblue

The wind blew the sun
and all the clouds away
Today.
And the sky alone
was blue, but not sad.
In fact,
I saw the canvas of creation
prompting my imagination.

## Spring Trees

Within the forest, I feel it
The everlasting Holy Spirit
Coaxing me and guiding me
To understand, what I see
There in the woods, a vibrant pink
From bad to good, one might think
Shrouded pain, its flowers white
Bled from shame, now pink in light
And then one hears the dogwood bark
Flowers of white that shred the dark
Nature's shadows turn away
Because each Spring, lights the way
Trees once silent, now take a breath
Blossoms life that fear no death
Within the woods, trees they stand
Reflected in the eyes of man
Rejoice, they sing, do not weep
In Spring is Life, say trees that speak.

*(According to legend, Judas hung himself from a redbud tree.
The redbud, which once had white flowers, bled, causing the
flowers to turn pink. I wrote this poem about the redbud tree
and the dogwood, the tree upon which Christ was crucified.)*

# A day at the end of March in Charleston, Tennessee

It rained last night and grass
glistens like glass
beneath the morning sun.
The birds make it clear
they are far and near.
The rolling hills tumble toward mountains
until stopped by rocky tops.
A red barn sits in the distance, atop fields of green
the owner's home, not seen,
acres away, in the woods or by a stream,
the past made present, from a dream.
As I walk through rural Tennessee,
I wonder if the word pastoral arose
from its country roads –
The word fits like denim, covered
with fertile dirt.

## Antiques

I treasure antiques.
They have survived.
They reflect craftsmanship
of another era
and wisdom
or errors in judgement.
They represent man's imperfection,
and simplistic precision,
and majestic ambition.
They display weathered beauty
and inspire memories.
They make me smile
when I hear them talk
because they
have stories to tell.
Time is their unforgiving partner
but the compelling guide
to whom they all abide.
I cherish many of them
and wish they do not perish,
but they will
eventually,
So I treasure them,
Intentionally.

## ode

mary loved waves and

meadow loved hills, maeve worked clay

mae elated by hay.


*(Inspired by "maggie and milly and molly and may" by e.e. cummings)*

## Something to consider

They say life's a play
So make each day the last act
Not dress rehearsal.

*(This Haiku arose from one of my favorite sayings from my best friend Nolan)*

## Daylight Savings Time

As a younger man
Time was afterthought. Older;
A day but seconds.

## A beautiful mind

I did my thesis
on Telekinesis,
and I suggest you sit down
to hear what I found.
I researched for years
between people's ears
and just to be fair
let me first clear the air,
by putting things right,
saying it's not black or white.
In fact, I will offer to say,
the data's more gray
though I have to admit,
when I ponder and sit
I am truly astounded,
and a little dumbfounded,
because what I have found
were minds truly profound.
Let me also state,
it would be a mistake,
to suggest as a man,
I now understand,
all that I saw,
as science has flaws.
And though I examined many who said,
they spoke with the dead,
or could, perhaps bend a spoon,
or move a chair in the room,
they were, sadly to say,
not a tiny bit gray.
In fact, all of these feats,
were more trick than a treat.

And their dark mysticism
aroused stark cynicism,
and undeserving of mention,
or further attention.

But the children I met
were something else yet;
Revealing to me
Ability,
To go beyond time,
And change paradigms,
Which fly in the face
Of societal grace.

I first found a boy,
Playing with toys,
When only just three,
Spoke, infinity.
And after telling you Hi,
He recited you Pi,
As far as we know,
As far as it goes,
Until it was enough,
We knew sure-enough,
His mind unencumbered,
Knew all of the numbers!
And as we were going,
He said "God is all knowing,"
As he smiled, and looked to the sky,
As we smiled, and said our goodbyes.
And when I walked to my car,
I stopped, and looked at the stars,
And wondered, how it could be,
He knew what he knew, at only just three.

I then met a girl,
In laces and curls,
Who was only nine,
But her skills divine,
As she could add and divide
what computers decide!
And she too, looked to the skies,
Though born without eyes,
I think she saw more,
Than ever before!
And her beautiful smile,
Seemed as long as a mile,
And I will never forget,
That girl that I met,
In ruffles and lace,
With such a sweet face,
And a soft little voice,
Which said to rejoice,
And reached to your soul,
Mending broken to whole,
And you knew that she cared,
And made you aware,
With calm in her tone,
That you're never alone.

I saw a young man,
Who was a big fan,
Of reading good books,
And whenever I looked,
I could see that he knew,
All, not a few,
Of the very first word,
Whether noun or a verb,
Of every book page,

Remarkable for one,
Of any an age.
He was just seven,
And had already read,
Three thousand eleven,
Books in his bed!
To it, his body confined,
But only it, and by grace,
Not even a trace,
of his far-seeing mind.
How is that possible, I wondered and asked?
To that he just smiled, and then we both laughed.
And all of a sudden, we turned to the skies,
And without ever asking, I understood why.

In all of my time, doing this study,
Was I never to find, a movable body,
Or books or tables, or vases or chairs,
Moving around, or floating in air,
But what I did see,
Was moving to me,
And what I did find,
Was an incredible sign,
That one human, exquisite, and beautiful mind,
Can alter and shape, the course of mankind!
So in summary, I would hazard a guess,
Perhaps a bit more, and not a bit less,
I believe that my thesis,
on Telekinesis,
Proved that in theory; it's certainly true,
That the mind of others, can surely move you.

*(Thank you, Dr. Seuss. The genius of your work continues to extend from one generation to the next and I hope it always will.)*

# I Wonder....

"He who has a why to live for can bear almost any how."

Friedrich Nietzsche

## Fissures

The body of land is
weakened by drought.
Green Trees drop yellow
leaves      which
drift
      slowly
to
     the
ground.
The leaves
of shrubs
            d
                 r
                    o
                      o
                        p
with sadness.
Pink blooms
collapse
onto
 the
ground, unwillingly.

Rain

  falls

and the sickness

consuming the body

is forgotten for a moment.

It is an antibiotic

injected into the roots

turning

a sallow pallor green

and

Melancholy to Hope.

## Trees

Even a tree,
has wounds,
broken limbs,
or a twisted image reflecting
a malformed shadow.

Yet, the weak, the hungry,
and lost find
comfort and beauty
in its earthy moods
every day.

## Dead Trees

The sky is gray today
as I walk through the woods.
I see a lot of dead trees still
standing, full of holes,
made by birds and bugs.
Their bark is more absent
than present and I wonder
what keeps them upright?
These trees will fall victim
to an unfriendly wind
or decay someday
but now, they are still there,
a blank stare, but visible.
I cannot be a dead tree,
Say I to I,
found standing on the ground.
I have to make my presence
known and found
for as long as I can be
and for as long as you can see.
Then when I am not,
and forgot from the woods,
in the mind,
you'll find I persist
for a little while longer.
In a dream or a stream,
or blade of grass,
that grows and flows
and last and lasts.

## A Wooded Path

As I walk through placid woods,
Evil works destroy good.
Shadows grow within the light,
They always will; that's why we fight.
It will win battles, here or there,
With innocence, victim, when we don't care.
But in these woods, I hold so dear,
I know that God, will calm my fear.
Never will I, forget to pray,
Or see the beauty, in another day.
Camellia's colors, a Lenten Rose,
A Daffodil, in stately pose.
Twisted oaks, and upright pines,
Provide to me, peace of mind.
My dog who walks with me each day,
Shows me when I go astray,
And with my eyes upon a wooded path,
My faith in God remains steadfast.


*(This poem was written at the beginning of the invasion of Russia into Ukraine. Wars take place all over the world and in a sense, we just accept them. I don't believe wars will ever end in our lifetime. I pray for the innocents and for peace but this idea of constant war is unsettling. It tests my faith and many days I retreat to the woods to find refuge.)*

## promises

Some trees hold their leaves longer.
Rust, ten-carat gold, maroon,
These colors suggest it is not time.
Time when bare trees remind bare souls
a sun will come and fill
their outstretched limbs with warmth.
There is so much color within the fall.
There is so much hope within the winter.
And the palette of spring takes your breath away.
I think when we swim in summer's light,
We sometimes forget
how beautiful
all the other days were,
And the promises each one held.

# A beautiful picture of winter

The bare trees of winter no longer filter the sun as well as they
do in the summer.
The shadows stand on the brown floor doubling the size of the
forest and the unique stature of each tree is heightened.
Broken trees lay on the ground with a new purpose.
Tiny pine saplings suggest Christmas but will grow into large
pillars of quilted bark with green pointed tops,
needles, and here and there, old bird nest hair.
The dry creek bed in the summer is awash with a tranquil
noise from days of rain and disappears into the earth's soul.
Pine needle pick-up sticks are thrown to the ground where
they become carpet with frayed edges on the road.
The Saw Palmettos engulfing the marsh look prehistoric.
Grand, Green Magnolias, Stand Tall and demand attention.
The red Nandina berries and Holly berries are tiny shiny
beacons for birds and anyone who sees them.
But the pink, candy cane, blood red, purplish red, Christmas
sleigh red, and white Camellia's, command center stage.
My feet ache from walking, but I don't want to stop
Because what was common, was never common.
So I walk a little more, painting the scene with my eyes
which becomes a beautiful picture of winter
and displayed in the museum of my mind.

## Winter walk

The sun shimmers in the sky.
The temperature is brisk, not cold.
The leaves, wet from yesterday's rain, soak up the warmth of
the sun.
A solitary Spirea hangs onto avocado green and mustard
yellow leaves for a little longer.
Walking on mounds of pine needles is like walking on brown
tufted pillows.
Tree stumps line the woods like tombstones honoring a lost
but never forgotten son or daughter.
Winter becomes a picture book
when we take the time and learn to look.

## A Winter Storm on the Horizon

The sky is dark and stormy gray
The stark treetops, bend and sway
The wolf-like winter wind howls
Rain pushes the air and pelts the ground
The degree of separation
between ice and water is small,
and I know frozen limbs tend to snap
and fall, so I pray for temperance.

## respite

I sought freedom in the forest but it was elusive as deer. I have come to realize I cannot separate the world in which I live from the world in which I walk, but I can find respite and deliberate thoughts and joy and beauty. So much beauty! I think it was arrogance, or ignorance, or perhaps both, to think I could escape the world.

Is it selfish? No. I don't think so, because I've become wise with my eyes and I simply retreat for a moment and embrace what is omnipotent, what is was, what will be, what is me for now.

## A Lifetime

"I can't remember when he's looked so good."
Really? You haven't seen him in a very long time
because he looked *better at home* alive.

Why do people say such things?
I suppose they are trying to be nice or
perhaps don't know what else to say
in these types of situations. Perhaps, it doesn't matter.

Those who loved him, are in a coma and hear little.
They just want It to be over.
They want a reboot on their lives.
They want him back.
They don't want to maneuver through
the next several weeks like they
are walking through a field of
land mines, where a song
or a picture, or a word,
explodes and they bleed grief.
Not again. It's what they want,
but they know It's not possible.
Not now.

Those who lost him will remember all the good times; Soon.
They will remember the life they shared; Again and again.
They will weep, and cry, but they will also smile and laugh.
They will Cry Immensely.
They will Laugh Intently.
And they will never forget.
For a lifetime, they will never forget
how love filled the air they breathed.

For a lifetime, they will never forget all the good times they had together.
And the pain will go away.
Not gone from every pore of their body,
but gone from the part of the body controlling
their ability to breathe and talk and carry on.
The pain will not consume them over their Lifetime as it does now.
And they will understand how we are each given a Lifetime.
And they will smile.


*(This poem arose from the death of a friend's husband. He died unexpectedly and was very young. I know she has put her best foot forward but I also know she still hurts. I grieve for her still.)*

## A moment in time

When he asked the question,
His button nose crinkled.

"Why is it grandpa, your skin is so wrinkled?"

I smiled, and looked into his brown eyes,
and sighed, as I lifted him on my lap.
"Well grandchild, this old skin's been out there
In a baking sun, working on the farm,
in the garden and the barn.
And just over time, living makes it so your skin gets more
thin, and doesn't seem to grow back as well as it used to."

"Oh," he said and nodded his bushy head.

And then he looked up again into my face,
And though cloudy, I could see the shape,
Of another question mark.

"Why is it grandpa, your eyes look so glassy and gray?"

I smiled, and looked into his brown eyes,
and sighed, as I shifted him from one knee to the other.
"Well grandchild, these old eyes, they've seen the world
for close to ninety years,
and I've looked at men with courage and looked at men with
fear, and laughed with both, and even shed a tear.
I've read a thousand books, the Bible every day,
I've seen the world around me dotted with a million bales
of hay.

And with all the seeing I've gotten done,
Well grandson, sometimes your eyes become like glass and
just a little gray."

"Oh," he said and nodded his bushy head.
And then I looked away for a moment,
And wondered where I was just then,
before I heard an angel's voice, talk to me again.

"Why is it grandpa, you sometimes can't remember?"

I smiled, and looked into his brown eyes, and sighed,
as I ran my hand through his bushy hair.
"Well grandchild, as I get older, my mind gets weighted
down, because of the memories on my shoulders.
And sometimes I forget a name or two, or a place or few.
But I promise you, even though things may never be the
same,
I won't ever forget those brown eyes, or my grandson's
name."

"Oh," he said and nodded his bushy head.
He smiled and hugged me, said he loved me,
And for a moment in time, they both saw faces in heaven.

## An old empty pickle jar

Firefly glowing in my jar,
I often ponder what you are.
Glowing there in the night,
Blinking on and off so bright.

Are you fairies, or little sprites?
Dancing all about the night.
Tell me Dad, what do you know?
About these things all aglow.

"It's not a fly at all. It's a beetle.
Order: Coleoptera.
Family: Lampyridae.
Genus:  Anadrilus, Araucariocladus,
Crassitarsus, Lamprigera,
Oculogryphus, Photoctus,
and Pollaclasis."

Ah shucks.
Knowledge is sometimes tragic.
When it takes away the magic.

*(This poem is essentially a reflection of my father. He was
very witty and funny. I think he would have liked this poem.)*

## The Lamp

I loved reading beneath my favorite lamp,
until I got tired of reading, so I did other things.
But as I got older, I realized I missed reading
beneath my favorite lamp.
So, I got some new books and settled in
and began reading again.

I enjoyed reading those new books every day
until my favorite lamp surged and the bulb
exploded. It scared me!
The master electrician said there was a short
in the wiring causing the misfiring, but he fixed it.
And my favorite lamp provided me with enough
light to read a hundred books, before I had
to replace the light bulb.

But the wiring became frayed and
and at times, I was afraid to turn on the lamp,
but I did anyway and it worked.
Until there was another surge and the master electrician said
it couldn't be fixed. But I still liked the way the lamp
looked so I sat there in my favorite chair, with my favorite
books, in my favorite nook beneath my favorite lamp, and
read during the day.

## Silent Night

His bed looked empty.
The other 99 beds in the
Cavern of unanswered echoes,
they called a ward,
Were full.
Sickness stained the walls,
and permeated the air like
smoke and soldiers were dying.
No one should die in a place like that;
even if there are 99 other brothers at your side.
I have never felt so helpless in my life;
though I hid behind a statue-like face of composure.
I know I projected that demeanor for her.
But perhaps, I did it for him too.
To let him know, I would be okay.
Fifty years later, I'm better.
In fact, you could say I am okay.
But I still see him in that bed;
And I still remember how
empty that bed looked
And how Empty I felt.

*(For my father, who died December 23 at the age of 53. I was 17 at the time. He was a gentle soul who died too early in life. I am still processing it as I think that's what we all do with the death of a parent, family member, or dear friend. We never get over it, we just process it. It is impossible for me to manage without the belief this world is not the end. It is only the beginning. Without that belief, I would process some deaths very poorly.)*

## Outer Space

The surgeon operated on her,
But it felt like he had stitched me up at 30,000 feet.
I stumbled out of my seat into the bathroom and
tried to breathe.
When I looked into the mirror all I could see was
the world was not as wide-open as it used to be.
I struggled to breathe.
Now, I try not to hurry into worry,
but my brain has disdain for wisdom.
So, death gets a whiff of my breath,
And again, I struggle to breathe.
Time is not a friend of mine.
Yet, there are sensations
of elation when problems are overcome
and to arise is less of a surprise and I am relieved
I can breathe.


*(This poem is about my mother's first diagnosis of colon
cancer. It was a very bad day.)*

## It's not easy to understand

Man's lack of humanity
Screams with insanity.
And makes you question why
Good people die.

The only way I can understand
Comes from words of a man
I consider very wise, who had eyes
That could ascend beyond the skies
And help us realize Why.

It's because there was more
Than one sacrifice that gave us life.
And even though I think I see,
It's still hard for me to understand man.
But in the end I don't have to.
I just need to see what God did for me,
And accept it willingly.


*"God created things which had free will. That means creatures which can go wrong or right. Some people think they can imagine a creature which was free but had no possibility of going wrong, but I can't. If a thing is free to be good it's also free to be bad. And free will is what has made evil possible. Why, then, did God give them free will? Because free will, though it makes evil possible, is also the only thing that makes possible any love or goodness or joy worth having." C.S. Lewis – The Case for Christianity*

## Brown eyes

Six-year-old eyes
Seldom see the skies.
They see the rain,
But not the pain,
In everyone who cries.

Little boys,
See their toys.
Older eyes,
See the skies,
And mountains and hills
Provide a thrill
At what is gained
By sweat and pain.

Boys become men
And become wise.
Is it when
They widen their eyes
To see the skies
For the first time
And wonder why?

## Behavioral Observation

Old dogs and old men are alike;

They both have to pee

in the middle of the night.

## Storms

I fear thunderstorms.
Those that destroy
what was standing
what was whole
what provides
Shelter or
Beauty or
Comfort.
I fear thunderstorms
because I cannot
control them.
I am told
what I cannot
control, I must accept.
I do not believe this.
I can control my fear
but it will require a
Thunderstorm of my
Own making.
Won't That be beautiful?
Won't That be heavenly?

**Suppose**

Old age isn't inevitable.

It should be desirable, but it isn't always.

Why isn't it for everyone?

Is it because of our frail human bodies and minds?

Is it because of increasing loneliness and grief?

Is it because our anxiety increases as the world around us and inside us is falling apart?

Is it because we have lost our will to survive?

There is only one way to live forever, but many of us wish to ignore how that is a remote possibility.

Disease has been present since time became time.

Hate, bigotry, lust, dishonesty, theft, cruelty, ignorance, and evil, are words familiar to man since time became time.

Love, respect, faith, truth, charity, friendliness, intelligence, and good, are words familiar to man since time became time.

So what do you think about when you wake up?

Do you recognize you are frail and determine how to be well, or do you become more fragile?

It's your choice.

Suppose it has been that way since time became time.

## Reading Glasses

Is your glass half empty or half full?
I am still debating this.
I reckon that response is optimism with a hint of pessimism.
Or it could be pessimism with a smidgen of optimism.
Perhaps there's nothing but blue skies on the horizon.
Or maybe, there's a storm a-brewin'.
I'm still chewin' on that.
I pray for the best, but fear the worse.
Is this a blessing or a curse?
I tend to be a half-full glass person when
blue skies are all I see.
I tend to be a half-empty glass person when
storms are bouncing off of me.
I think there should be more consistency within my eyes.
Yes, I realize that.

## Confinement

The cavern is a labyrinth of painful stalactites which may fall down.
You hear gurgling sounds in the dark, and the water doesn't smell clean. It smells old. Contaminated. But contaminated by what?
You notice your breathing is labored because you do not like the dark claustrophobic feeling.
Anxious echoes reverberate within the structure more stricture than structure. All you can do is sit down and breathe.
Breathe through the dark, and hope the lamp on your miner's helmet does not go out. When it flickers, you take a deep breath and tap your helmet.
The light stays on. For now.
Is it easier to get out of the cavern by going back to where you were, or is there an unseen opening through the dark extending out beyond the light?
You push yourself up off the ground and stand up.
Which way do you go?
Follow the light you tell yourself when you turn your head, and realize the light goes both ways.


*(I suffer from severe diverticular disease. This was a bad time in my life and the day before, the day of, and the day after a procedure to evaluate the progression of the disease.)*

**Reflections**

I wonder whose face it is
looking at me in an odd manner.
I have seen it before but I
don't remember when
and then, I remember.
The fast of the past
And the how of the now.
As I look out the window,
I see the trees
And close my eyes
And wonder why
I chase tomorrow
and sigh about time I borrow.
I then bow my head
and try to focus
on now instead.


*(I just had a squamous cell cancer removed from my face and then was told I had another one that needed to be removed. I needed to find comfort. God is a very good listener and it's amazing how once we learn to listen, the answers we seek can be heard.)*

## A summer day

Though I started the flower garden almost a year ago, it is far from done as I try to manage the water and sun. The plants, preferring full sun, were not consulted when placed into a full sun setting for summers in Augusta. It exceeds their expectations. I am learning though. What was a patchy field of grass and weeds is now a patchy field of golden yellow sedum, dragons blood sedum, and autumn sedum.

In a corner of the garden, there is a double feature drive-in show of fire red and yellow, maroon and yellow, magenta and yellow, ruffled pink, sunset orange, and pale pink and lime green daylilies. There are small mounds of light blue lavender, Russian blue sage, and dark blue hummingbird mint aligning the rocks providing the backdrop for the garden.

White and gold water lilies, a few yellow coneflowers, a maroon gaillardia, pink yarrow and blue veronica have bloomed since spring. There is an Indian hawthorne and a false yew and a yellow holly next to small boulders and a daphne in the shade of the large crepe myrtles.

There are two butterfly twiggy Japanese maples but the leaves are still beautifully variegated. Dahlias have a wealth of dark crimson leaves and an agapanthus has a waterfall of green leaves but neither plants have bloomed. They are not yet neighbors.

There is a flagstone rock path meandering through the flowers, velvet green moss, and unwanted grass and weeds. One day, I will say, the garden is full of flowers and beautiful ground cover throughout the year. But weeds will thrive in wet or dry soil or full and partial sun and so I am not done.

I long for a garden with fewer weeds and more beauty. Some say weeds have beauty. They are green but I cannot find the beauty in them when they seek to strangle their neighbor's neck. They are ill-mannered and though they will never cease to exist, I can minimize their voice so it is barely a whisper and ignored.

In fact, I refuse to allow them to disrupt the serenity and the beauty of the garden. I will outlast them.

## A Prayer

i need to retreat to the woods to heal my intestinal fortitude
it needs to be rebuilt
i need to cut tree limbs and dig in dirt and plant flowers and
dig up weeds
the red hot poker is there in the garden
perhaps i can use it to fuse the holes in my body
perhaps, i can fill in the holes with green, wet moss, and mud
i am so tired
but i need to work outside
because i am not sure how many more outsides there will be
i welcome a thousand more in the hot sun
as opposed to hours of mental uncertainty
in air-conditioned walls failing to protect me
my body and the woods converse
the voice is distant now
but welcome
i fear when the conversation ends
the rocks will weep
i pray my toes become roots
and I am grounded
as i see more storms forthcoming


*(This poem arose after experiencing diverticulitis. **I** do not
wish that on anyone.)*

## Moss

I walked deep into the woods today in places I have never
been before
The dark rainy disposition of the air was not unlike my own
mood I exhaled
The dirt was different shades of brown, some dry, but most
wet and becoming mud
I longed to see the moss, the green carpet, like man, needing
water to survive
It prefers the shade, and at times, shuns the light, but is
aware, it cannot live without glances
I understand its temperament; in fact, I sometimes share it.

It is an ancient form of life
and continues to thrive in harsh environments
Hell, it can grow on rock.
Though rootless, it gives nature feet when there are none
It creates a habitat enabling other plants to grow
It provides shelter to animals
It adds color to the world
I want to be moss.

## Shadow land

I sought out the woods again today
and went farther into them than the day before
The only sound I heard was thunder
The inhabitants of the woods were silent
aware of the coming storm
It began to rain but I didn't care
as I enjoyed hearing the rain drip through the trees
I was in a wooded area, old with many ferns and
saw palmettos and various green shades of moss
growing along the muddy path, sometimes a stream
The wooden deacons stood tall and welcomed me into the
wall-less church with the celestial stained glass and earthen
floor
I walked in a spiritual shadow land and the pain within my
body became numb by the beauty in the silence of the rain.

## A hot summer day

It was a hot summer day and I went deep into the woods. The sun made you remember what summer in the south is like but the woods were shaded and provided relief from the heat. I took a seat on a tree stump and looked around, listening to the sounds flying all around me.

Oreo watched me from the edge of the woods. She no longer goes into the woods like she did without fear when she was a younger dog. She does not like flying things when I walk into woods unpopulated by man.

I looked at the large trees and the mossy sheen and plants of green. I turned and saw hundreds of ferns as if they had been planted there on a hillside with purpose. There were two large oaks grown together with a large root, a bridge that made both trees more steady when the ground in which they were rooted was underwater. I thought how beautiful everything looked, untouched and unfiltered but I knew I needed to get home as it was a hot day, and for my older dog, was reason to pause for her paws.

As I walked out of the woods, Oreo wagged her tail and I started heading home. I looked back for a moment, and I saw her nose in the air, the beagle in her wanting to stop and check out the grass growing along the road. I continued home and when Oreo emerged from the grass I was nowhere to be seen, so she followed the scents of our daily walks and went down the road away from home. I think her younger self would have not been confused but I am not sure.

My neighbor called me within minutes and said Oreo was at her house, which she had never been to before, and was rummaging through their garage. I got in the car and drove to their house. Oreo came running, happy to see me and jumping all over me. She smiled (though others may say she was panting). I saw the smile on her face even though I also saw the fear in her eyes until it disappeared when she got in the car and was sitting next to me. I asked her if she thought she was a young puppy going on big adventures. She smiled again and I remembered when.

I wondered if my neighbor would have to call my wife someday because I had wandered down the road because it was something I remembered as familiar. Some might say a sad thought but I thought not. I am aware of the pain and agony people endure when their family members are no longer sure about who, what, when, where, or why, and I too cry for them and with them. How, not now, we always say almost every day. I know all we can do during those times is be there, tell them you are here, they are here, and not to fear. We can say it but we know it falls on deaf ears many times; theirs and ours.

But there are moments when the light shines from their eyes onto your face as they retrace a memory and a bond remains and we refrain from crying. In fact, we talk and smile and remember for a while, better times and love fills the room again, for those times when.

I hope I am always able to remember what is good – the Good road I have walked thousands of times, the Good woods, the Good flowers, the Good trees, the Good black and white dog, the Good family, the Good friends familiar to me when I can't see what is familiar or everywhere I look, I'm lost in a book I can't read. But I can cope with a hope knowing even a sliver of a memory of what is Good will provide me glimpses into Heaven.

## The First Day of September

I sit outside and watch it rain
The dogwood on the hill
is filled with red berries
and the leaves are dusted rust.
Seasons changing.
I pause for a moment
because I'm a component
of the transformation.

## There in the air somewhere

Sighing is better than crying when Oreo
bites the air at flies not there.
She has a condition known as fly biting syndrome,
a rare canine condition of unknown etiology.
Seizures and hallucinations cause agitation and we pray the
medications we keep trying will bring
cessation to this condition.
Some help, but still she suffers and sometimes when I look to
her sad eyes I cannot keep my sighs
from falling down my cheeks.
I say it will be okay today and okay the next day and okay
each day and I pray she hears what I say.
I say it for her as I try and reassure myself it will be okay.

**one**

the words are a breeze ruffling the leaves
the soil feels good as I walk in the woods
which hold a small part of my body and heart and in which I
can find I lose track of time
for all I see are pictures to be beautiful and broken
silent unspoken green and unseen
brown without sound sky for the eye
a newly found friend alone in the wind

## Working in the garden and woods is good for the soil

Weeds choke the promise of beauty from the garden and it is my desire to pull out the weeds from the body of the ground. I need to be careful or I will pull out what I wish to keep like the golden sedum, cranberry sedum, daylilies, or curcuma lilies. It is a balancing act unless you accept the fact weeds will always be present and you must find some level of harmony with the unwanted. I am undaunted and persist so the garden will exist.

When I see dead limbs on the tree, I cut them off and cast them off into the woods. When dead limbs have fallen onto the floor of the woods, I cut them up and place them in a dark corner of the woods hidden, and eventually a part of the woods again. And then I realize, I can live in harmony with weeds but only if they serve a purpose in the woods as a shelter or as food for what lives there and away from the beautiful flowers and shrubs and trees bringing such pleasure to me. I tolerate fewer neighbors in my garden. The garden is beginning to teach me greater patience and tolerance is needed and will not exist unimpeded. Perhaps, I will live long enough to understand the garden's plan.

## A recent airport visit

I worry about society's grace
When I no longer see her face
Eyes that look down at a phone
Make me feel so all alone
Or eyes that look afraid and scared
Make me question what we share
I long for nice and kind and smiles
If not all day, just a while.

## Van Buren Arkansas

Before dawn becomes dawn,

the hint of a new day

provides a clue to the puzzle awaiting us.

I find I am unable to complete the picture when I wake up.

Perhaps one day, I'll be able to piece everything together.


*(We stayed here overnight on the journey back from Oregon on our 43rd anniversary trip, and then drove all the way to Augusta, Georgia the next day. It was a grueling fifteen-hour trip.)*

## 600 more miles on a 2500 mile trip completed in 4 days

Music transformed tired into a smile

for a while,

and I'll thank God when this road trip ends

and a new journey begins

with family and friends

and with a black and white dog

who leads me down the road in our neighborhood.


*(Another reflection on the trip back from Oregon)*

## Solitary

I saw a solitary house on a solitary rock
Over-looking a giant ocean
and I wondered
who in the world
would have a dream
to be so alone
in a home
on a giant stone?
As I stood there,
and questioned this thought
I began to see, maybe it was me,
and the appearance of solitary
was an arbitrary notion
from the rock and the ocean
isolated by eyes
failing to pause
to seek a cause
for such a life.
I saw a solitary path
Leading straight to a solitary wooden gate
Surrounding a field of iridescent fireweed
with grasses, green and brown
filling in other parts of the ground.
I saw the weathered wood on the home, gray
conjuring fog and mist
with storms twisted against it.
Yet,
this solitary home
defied the weather
or whether
anyone like me
suggesting its location, was so brazen.

I saw a weathered man
take a stand
on his weathered porch
and stare into the air
and I again wondered
who would choose
such a solitary view?
Were they just contrary
being solitary
or was it fate
which chose this slate
and have a notion
to view the ocean?
I questioned
if this solitary man
viewed the world
as I saw the world
and I knew
he could not
from his isolated spot
and I felt sorry
for such isolation
and then
I saw the man smile
as he sat on his porch
for a while
and I did not understand
this man at all.
As I stood there
processing what I saw,
I wondered
if there was something
I didn't see
or didn't know,

as he looked
at the sea
and tidal flow.
Perhaps,
I will return
to this solitary home
on this isolated stone
and go down
the private path
to the wooden gate
and wait.
And buy this lot
on such a beautiful spot
and then one day
I can say,
I looked out
into oceans vast,
and found the answers
others asked.


*(This poem was inspired by looking at some of the homes on the Oregon coastline. They were just there with nothing else around them but mountains, beach, and ocean. Amazing homes that seemed perfect and out of place at the same time.)*

## Rainy day walk

It was raining when Oreo and I walked this morning and though it is August in Augusta, it did not feel like a jungle. The weather was pleasant and the rain slowly dropped onto the hood of my jacket and onto the fur of Oreo.

I enjoyed hearing the rain fall through the trees. It was the only sound I heard besides Oreo tapping her paws against the wet leaves.

I am not sure a year ago I would have even considered going out for a walk on a day like this and now I understand how much I miss nature when I am not in its midst. She presents herself to us every day. She can be furious and unforgiving and when she is, we need to respect her and protect ourselves from her rage.

But, when she opens the door for you and invites you to come outside, one would be a fool not to listen to her. Take the advice from a former fool.

## Some things never get old

I walk with my little black and white dog this morning.

It is beautiful beneath a cyan blue and chiffon white sky.

The trees and plants are still wet from rain the night before.

The dry creeks are full and rushing forward.

My body is enriched by the environment and a wholesome mood.

We are stupid animals with regard to our health

ignoring it when there is no problem

not aware having no problem

is a scientific and engineering endeavor

inimitable within the world.

Yet, we go by each day without concern

as if miracles are commonplace.

Do not take your health for granted

and give thanks for each day you are well.

One would be an idiot to do otherwise.

Unfortunately, I know a thing or two about idiots.

I have seen one in the mirror more than once

especially when I was younger,

and though not always the case

age has provided me some wisdom

along with a body that is an eloquent educator.

## Shoveling dirt

The walk this morning has hints of fall and though it is far from that season, the breeze is reason enough to have leaves floating to the ground yellow and brown.
When we return home, I shovel dirt and move rocks in the garden.
I see the transformation taking place, and flowers I planted, replacing the weeds which took for granted my less than vigilant nature.

When I was a young man required to mow the lawn every Saturday, I did not want to have anything to do with grass or flowers or plants and especially dirt.
But when I had my own place for the first time, something inside said I need to shovel some dirt.
I have been doing so ever since and am glad I listened.

## Waves

I lost a friend, not sure when but it was a time when sadness wrestled with madness and being grown fought alone

We saw many changes together and apart and I wouldn't know where to start to name them all for the promise of tomorrow is today and I will not let that get in the way with everything that I have to say

For in the end it doesn't matter

I just know it is sadder to say goodbye instead of hi

# Joy

I sit on the porch and listen to the waterfall and think how wonderful it sounds. The October day is beautiful and full of sun and soft temperatures. I think about how every day is a gift and then I wonder what if everything you loved to do, was suddenly taken away from you? What if what brings you joy was taken away from you, would it destroy you?

I hear a familiar refrain meander through my brain: Tomorrow isn't promised to you so enjoy the moments of now. So, I ask another question. What if you couldn't do what you used to do because of an accident or illness then how would you enjoy now? I think about the question and I remember a lesson I once learned about free will and how the choices we make determine our fate. I wonder if I will be strong enough to move through so much loss or if I will be tossed into a vast abyss.

The only way I can see how I can move away from depression and aggression and sadness and madness is because I know even with the dark's ferocity, hope remains a possibility. But still, I ask myself, will I be able to face such a test of my faith? And again, I hear familiar words. God has a plan even if we don't understand it, not sometimes, but all the time – thus the case for faith.

I have asked these questions a lot lately due to age and those I love dying or becoming very ill and because my chronic illnesses test my will more than ever before. And I wonder, why are these concerns the key opening the door to those notions in my mind when they aren't there when everything is fine?

I have asked the question before but it seems I cannot escape it so I should embrace it. Because it's a circular argument and the answer is the same every time. Tomorrow isn't promised to you so enjoy the moments of now. Joy can only be harnessed by the moment you're in; that's where everything begins.

I know those words are easier said than deeds done, and perhaps I've just begun to learn how a story is told as one continues to write each day of their life. But it would be a sorrow-filled world for me if joy in this world was the end of joy forever. I truly believe all art is work and all work is art when it involves a part of the heart. Hence the question again, what do you do when joy is taken away from you and I hear a voice coaxing me to remember: You have free will to have joy still. You just have to find the will to conquer the fear it will end here and now and find how to find yourself in it again. So, I pray every day to be better than the day before but unfortunately, it doesn't always happen.

Because of free will; I struggle with it still, but I am making progress.

## Changing of the Guard

The old brown dog has changed color.
The will to jump onto the familiar chair or sofa is restrained
as if she knows there are only so many jumps in a day.
At night the limp worsens and there is an inclination to lay
down without walking any farther than necessary.
Time reveals the frailty of life to me through another window
and I am a reluctant but attentive and wistful observer.

## Reunion

I stepped back in time yesterday

I hugged friends I hadn't seen in fifty years

We didn't talk long but we didn't have to

The smiles I saw will last a lifetime

The sparkle in their eyes reflected a child's wonderment, a magician's skill and tenacity which belies the fragile nature of his work, and a mystic's awareness to unlock the door of time connecting past, present, and future requires a key not available to everyone

The sun the next day was bright and though my shadow lengthened

Those brief moments of joy will forever lift my spirit and provide comfort against the bitter cold

## Fifty-one weeks ago

I hear water tapping on padded ground as ice melts.
It is calm, unlike fifty-one weeks ago when my dog and wife
and I encountered chaos.
We are better now, but have not forgotten the storm.
Memories linger which cause us fear we never knew.
At first, the woods are without song but as the sun's blanket
warms us, winged voices erupt.
The red bird, wren, warbler, finch, and thrush welcome us
along the wooded path.
I give thanks for this day but am troubled by a storm
lingering over another.
She will need steady hands to navigate through the
emotional downpour and I pray the winged chorus she hears,
will be as clear as the one my dog and I encountered today.

## Solace

The sun streamed through the silent trees this morning.

The weather was cool but with a jacket and hat, felt wonderful.

Magenta azaleas provided a surprise for the eyes within the green and brown, the primary colors now, but even so, the woods provide a unique landscape each time I see them.

Twisted trees and tree limbs appear to have been drawn onto a blue canvas and I stop and admire the artist's skill.

Oreo and I walk slowly.

She is drawn into the woods frequently by something she smells.

She chases a squirrel for a moment which makes me smile as her gait has been hindered of late.

The woods provide comfort and clear my mind for a while,

but I am still troubled by the grief consuming a loved one.

I pray she finds Solace soon.

## A Fall Prayer

The wind blows cold through the woods
beneath a cool white sky.
Crumbled brown leaves hang stubbornly on trees where now
verdant magnolias and olive green pines and emerald green
ligustrums command my attention.
Dogwood trees radiate color with orange
and apricot and maroon.
A hornbeam covered with lime green leaves makes me think
of a magnificent ball gown as its limbs hang down toward the
ground covering its feet and I admire the southern debutante
who chose such a bold dress to wear to the fall ball.
As I walk, a flashlight of sky turns on as the sun, once hidden
by a powder-white curtain, makes its presence known.
Being here in this moment is important and I am thankful I
have learned to see.
I pray the wind takes my prayers through the air to those I
care for deeply.

## Not long ago

A walk when the temperature is near freezing gives me
reason to pause because of her
Similar temperatures earlier this year help these days appear
normal and allow me to see
little diamonds of water glistening atop the leaves
A road is striped gray and white by the sun and trees
The woods are glorious on a cold, calm canvas
There is stillness in the air unlike earlier this year
when a storm brought her harm
and walked us down a road to recovery.

This road goes a long way
but we travel it every day
and I've learned to pray
for one day more
we can walk the road together.

# I will miss him

My brother-in-law passed away yesterday
He was sick for many years
Many tears were shed by those who loved him
We ask ourselves why those we love suffer so
And I really don't know the answer
But I believe He suffers too
Along with me and you
Especially for those who have a kind heart
And my brother-in-law had one of those
Even curmudgeons have them I suppose
He loved the woods and today
When my dog and I walked the wooded path
I saw him everywhere
In the trees and leaves
With the birds and squirrels
With the evergreens
With the encore azaleas
And in the arms of the sun
And clear blue sky
I will miss him.


*(For Tom and my sister Cathy)*

## little is better than none and more is better than little

a smoky gray morning
rain is everywhere
but we are warm and dry in our house
not everyone can say so
rain soaks the soul
but does not dampen the spirit of Hope
i cannot control rain but i can
provide coats to the soaked
but in the end it will rain again
a million times a million times, drops of rain
will drench and soak many more again
so why bother
a coat is false hope
one might say
and perhaps a coat will not help everyone
but it will help someone
which is better than none

## Ghosts

I'm not at all afraid to boast
About the fact I see a ghost.
I don't see them all the time
Which for them, I think is fine.
They'd be sad and maybe mad
If all the past and what was had
That was special with them and me
Was something every day I'd see.

They much prefer to be quite subtle
And not become such a trouble
That the past became my present
Every moment with their presence.

No, just a smile on a face
Or a moment in a place
Or perhaps a radio song,
Will be the prompt to come along
To a memory there in time
Stored forever in my mind
And my ghost is sitting there
Ethereal within the air.

And I smile for just a while
And remember, times compiled.
And should I happen to shed a tear
My ghost reminds me they're always near.
And when they know, they'll disappear
And come back, I have no fear,
Even though I may sadly sigh
To once again say goodbye.

Holidays will bring them round
And over the years I have found
They fill my heart again with love
My ghost that I am thinking of.
And with all the gifts spread 'round the tree
They will not, scare the dickens, out of me.
No! When I see them, with spirits soaring,
I have an Ebenezer Christmas morning!
And so again, I proudly boast,
And welcome all my many ghosts.

## Wisps

Wisps of clouds
Amidst the blue
Crows in crowds
And then there's you
Jasmine yellow all around
Falling silent to the ground
Camellia's colors still abound
As spring begins, to make a sound
Fingers of trees
Becoming leaves
Daffodils, align the creek
Little beacons in wooded deep
With woods so full, I wonder why
My breath exhales a solemn sigh
Body and mind do not speak
When one feels well, the other's weak
And then a neighbor stops to talk
As I am welcomed on my walk
And that neighbor on this day
Makes apathy wisp away
Just a simple neighbor's face
Fills a foolish empty space
And I learn, once again
His spirit heals a broken limb.

## The next morning when most people are at work

My dog's eyes speak and say
Take me for a walk today.
I take her out, even though
My tiny steps are very slow.
It's not too far, a step or two,
But she somehow knows,
That's all I'll do.
So she does what she needs to do
And with her eyes, asks how are you?
We go inside and take a chair,
She's next to me sitting there
and lays her head on my chest
knowing it's better if we rest.
I get up and go back to bed,
Oreo there, by my head.
And I wonder, if she knows,
Roles reversed four months ago,
When I lay with her on the floor
Because her pain would allow no more.
Though in pain and with a little fear,
I give thanks she is here.

# Unexplained

"Why love, if losing hurts so much? I have no answers anymore: only the life I have lived. Twice in that life I've been given the choice: as a boy and as a man. The boy chose safety, the man chooses suffering. The pain now is part of the happiness then. That's the deal."

C. S. Lewis

## mud

i walk in the dirt
my body filled with hurt
the woods fill up with rain
my stomach twists in pain
i fear to move my feet
or walk or take a seat
as I feel the mud
watery like my blood
dripping down my skin
afraid it will never end
i try to walk back home
but there i am alone
i fear the open streets
with strangers i have to greet
afraid of rain bringing a flood
and staining my body again with mud
i seek a path welcoming soles
i seek a path to make me whole
for the moments i cherish most
begin to feel like they are ghosts
and then I see the baby smile
and want to go another mile

**Daisies**

Angry words pelt others like a Hell storm.

I pray for better weather every day

and soon the Sun's presence

allows the clouds of frustration to dissipate

and I am no longer clinically defined as a lunatic.

I think I should plant more daisies and follow their lead.


*(I wasn't aware daisies follow the sunlight until I read a gardening magazine. The knowledge was there when I needed to address a bad day.)*

## Lofty Dreams

I stood among giants over three hundred feet tall, a thousand
years old
I was a fragile being beneath the shadows of majestic beings
in awe at what I saw
There were ghosts who stood among those trees but they
were not lost
They were there in the air we breathed
Old trees, big as wooden ships, lay aground on the fern
barnacles growing up around them
It was a holy path which I followed
Perhaps if we only knew we wouldn't have built an avenue
through this forest
But because someone needed wood, we could and we did
So now, we should listen to the silence of these ancient giants
because all they ask of man, is we understand
and leave no evidence of our presence.

*(On our trip to Oregon, we went into part of the Sequoia
forest. Yes, they were majestic and so beautiful, but I saw
signs all around saying, "don't do this or that because it is
hurting the ecosystem and killing the trees." Imagine that.
They built a road through the damn forest! Why? Can't we
hike to see them? I would have. Yes, I know some people can't
hike, so, how do we accommodate them? I bet we could find
a way for them to see these gentle giants, without building a
two-lane road through the middle of the forest.)*

## Monterey Bay

Seals lumber back and forth and bark on the rocks of Monterey Bay.

They lie in the sun and sleep on the rocks as hundreds of gawkers stare down on them.

My dog doesn't like lying on rocks but she likes lying in the sun in our bay window and sleeping.

She barks when aroused by the UPS, or FedEx, or USPS folks who knock on our door.

Perhaps the seals see us all as UPS, or FedEx, or USPS folks because we all wear similar uniforms.

Perhaps, that's why they bark too because we did not ask them to come near their bay window either.

## Variation

There's something in the air
Vacant stares everywhere
Affecting many, affecting few
Avoiding me, avoiding you
What are we supposed to do?
The world still plays and sings its songs
But what is right and what is wrong?
I'm not sure what to do
Except care for me and care for you.
I don't think we as man
Can control what we don't plan.
War, disease, endless strife
Have been with us all our life.
What happens next, I am afraid to ask
But perhaps the future reflects the past,
And what we think may be the end
Is the way the world, begins again.

## What next

A world without faces
Is full of dark spaces.
Faceless children is a world not free
And not a world I wish to see.
To think a mask becomes the norm
Would make me wish I wasn't born.
This virus is not a disease.
It is a symptom of our ill at ease
Standing there with each other
Smiling at strangers who are brothers.
I pray with all my beating heart
We find within us, a way to start.
Dismiss divisive and try to see
How we regain humanity.

**The sky was dark and gray before the sun came out**

When the person died why did no one cry?

No one ever came to confirm what was his name

Though the coroner was able to find who it was that died

He had been alone living in an abandoned house

They call it a pauper's burial which sounds improper

And the least amount of kindness for our deliberate blindness

For someone who had hidden in plain view of us

lonely and suffocating,

and I wonder if that is what took his breath away?

## Sadness in the air

Manure on the farm has purpose
excrement on pavement does not
We disrespect the land and We disrespect man
stepping over them as they lay there on the ground
as if We don't see them
They disrespect themselves for feeble reasons
and forceful reasons
but either way
We need to change the season of discontent
and the reasons for contempt.
Sadness permeates the air we breathe
and though We may want to, We cannot leave
because if We do, We may be through.
I pray We will find our souls again
and be able to say, remember when.

## Pray

I empathize with the earth's disruptive force
At times my body mimics its behavior
But the beautiful nature of the world exceeds the ugliness
everywhere
Hopefully for the sake of us, it will not forsake us.

## Connections

My gut reminds my mind
who is in charge periodically and methodically.
My dog's agitation worsens the situation.
My gut is in a rut but when my dog and I walk in the woods
life stops for a moment
because the woods are potent medicine for both of us.
I see the magenta and coral azaleas,
yellow and white wildflowers, the names I do not know
but how they glow along the side of the road.
There are rust-colored mushrooms,
alabaster white mushrooms,
reddish orange mushrooms,
popping up from the ground,
which I am not sure I would have found
months ago, but I see them now
and they allow me to escape
and reshape my consciousness
and breathe a sigh of relief.

# A funny looking Owl

A funny looking Owl on top
of the theater
stares down at me.
Every day I walk beneath
It, as
I go to work.
I see its claws dug
into the stone to keep it
from falling.
I wonder
if it stares down
at other people as
I go into my
cubicle
and turn on
my computer.
The manager comes by
and asks me
"how's it going?"
I look up at him
and smile
and say
"great" with
a gargoyle grin.
I look at the clock
and the time anchors
me to my chair.
I look forward to seeing
the funny looking
Owl on the way home,
and try and avoid
the pellet
The Owl vomits.

# Bliss

"Little Red Riding Hood was my first love. I felt that if I could have married Little Red Riding Hood, I should have known perfect bliss."

Charles Dickens

## Hand me downs

"Babies are amazing"
I heard my mother say
"Especially when you're 'a-raising
One of them someday!"
So I did what she suggested
And had a little boy,
And never once regretted
Or experienced so much joy!
"Babies are amazing"
Our son heard from his mother
And replied "I'll be 'a-praising
The day I am a father."
"Babies are amazing"
I hear my son now say
"And it's a joy to be 'a-raising
My daughter every day!"
"Grandbabies are amazing"
Alex heard his mother say,
"A blessing worth 'a-praising
When I hold sweet Joan each day!"

## First Time

I hold a star in my hand
No easy feat for any man.
My heart it glows and blurs my eyes,
When I hold the sparkling sky.

It is a blessing to hold a star
Before it goes away too far.
The smile it gives to wrinkled hands,
Gives pleasure to all who understand.

I will forever hold it dear,
For as long as star and I are near.
And when time fades, I will not cry,
For I held a star beneath my eyes.

## Sigh

Time stops for a moment
when you smile
and past and present
become one,
when I see my son
in your grin.
And then,
Gerbers and giggles
And granddaughter
Become words I can use
To describe you.
What a lucky guy am I
To hear a baby sigh
Again.

## Wish

I wish for you a world
In which you can be free
I wish for you a world
Of truth and honesty

I wish for you a world
In which you can grow strong
I wish for you a world
Where neighbors get along

I wish for you a world
Where hard work enjoys success
I wish for you a world
Where you always give your best

I wish for you a world
Of wisdom and of health
I wish for you a world
With no poverty, just wealth

I wish for you a world
Of literature and art
I wish for you a world
That doesn't tear apart

I wish for you a world
Where you visit all the seas
I wish for you a world
Of beauty you can see

I wish for you a world
Where you hear the birds and bees
I wish for you a world
Filled with mountains and many trees

I wish for you a world
With nature as your guide
I wish for you a world
Filled with musical asides

I wish for you a world
Where promises are fulfilled
I wish for you a world
Of journeys full of thrills

I wish for you a world
Where you make the most of time
I wish for you a world
Where you are charitable and kind

I wish for you a world
Full of many friends
I wish for you a world
With joy from day to end

I wish for you a world
In which you can find love
I wish for you a world
With a family you can hug

I wish for you a world
Full of a virtuous belief
I wish for you a world
To know healing comes from grief.

I wish for you a world,
And I wish for you the most,
You will always love yourself,
And God, who loves you most.

## Floating on a Cloud

"Slept like a baby"
is a beautiful phrase,
especially to those
who witness
it firsthand,
looking down on,
tiny hands.

## Moment

You stopped in for a short while
But a fast hour of smiles
Lasts a long time and become heartbeats.
They were there the next day and the next.
I wait again
For you to stop in
For a short little while
With an hour of smiles
I'm certain I'll see,
Will be forever with me.

## A Walk in the Woods

As I walked in the woods one day

I was startled when it came my way!

A rabbit ran across the road

and stopped

looked at me and prepared to hop

should I move a tiny step

so I stood there very silent

and unmoving, just admired it.

And I thought about a palace

And the girl I knew as Alice

And I wondered if our grand

Not yet flowing with golden strands,

Would one day too, see that bunny

And imagine it just as funny

As we remembered its storied fate

"Oh dear, oh dear, I shall be late"

And we would both, laugh out loud

Our laughter a signal, three's a crowd!

And then the bunny, would dart away

For us to see, another day.

As we continued with our talk

Of magic mirrors understood,

On a walk in the woods.

## One Day

I hope to take you on a plane
and fly through clouds and sky-blue air

Soaring off to here and there
and maybe a place, who knows where?

We'd fly across the mountaintops
and find someplace we'd want to stop

To spend a day or night or two,
never wondering what we must do.

We'd fly across the oceans blue
and stop a while if we wanted to

and walk the beaches without shoes
and wonder where we've gotten to

or maybe even fly in space
and give the moon a warm embrace!

Yes, I'd like to take you to these places,
but it all depends on holy graces.

But, if we flew with our words,
we could fly as free as birds,

and go wherever we want to go,
and go whenever we want to go,

Because in our minds we truly know,
there's not a place we couldn't go!

## Words

"What are you?" she asked, in a curious way.

"A word" said the word, "now go outside and play!"

"But there are more than one of you, there are many others too," she said.

"Of course," replied the word, "we're a poem that's being read."

"A po-em?" she repeated, in a questionable way.

"What is a po-em of words, really going to say?"

"It's a poem not po-em," the word said with haste,

"And a poem is where the words, have a special place

to tell us a story, a feeling, or a thought

and sometimes they may rhyme

and sometimes, they may not."

"Really?" asked the girl, with interest in her smile,

"Can I read the poem, with you for just a while?"

"Hmmm," said the word, "would you rather not go play

then listen to whatever, a poem has to say?"

"I can go play later," the girl said with glee,

"Please take this pretty poem, and share it all with me!"

"Okay," said the word, "but listen with great care,

as the words begin to float, slowly through the air

and drift into your ears and all throughout your mind,

where you can see the words, of a magic kind,

where some may make you laugh, or perhaps may touch your heart,

so, are you sure you are ready, to give it all a start?"

"Yes," said the girl, and then she looked surprised,

For she found that she was reading, the poem beneath her eyes!

## The Eating Suit

My granddaughter has an Eating Suit
For sticky rice and sticky fruit,
Otherwise, she'd use a spoon
But I'm afraid, it's a tad bit soon
To move the food, that's on the spoon
Into her mouth, without most of it
Falling south, or lots of it
Into her seat, or onto feet
So that is why, the Eating Suit
Is really neat
And eating food is no big feat!
'Cause now she eats, with her hands
Which makes perfect sense, you understand!
And eating rice with your hands
Makes the Eating Suit, a high demand!
And when she dons her Eating Suit,
And gets into her Eating seat,
She'll make a sound, like a hoot,
Meaning – "I'm going to soon, get to eat,
Some tasty rice or juicy fruit!"

I think I'll get an Eating Suit,
So when they say it's dinner time,
She'll wear hers and I'll wear mine
And we'll both have, the best of times!
Sitting there in our Eating Seat
Gnawing something good to eat
Not worrying at all, about our clothes
Or if the food, goes up our nose
Or falls back down on the floor
Cause there's always a little more
We can find, on our Eating suit,
Covered with rice and juicy fruit!

## One going on two

When I look into your face,
I see your father,
Who like you,
Was a good thief too.
When I see you smile,
I see your father smile,
And it takes me back a while,
To many days of joy,
When he was just a boy.
How wonderful a day can be
That allows for me, again to see,
Him in you again.
Your smile steals my heart
And now a part of you,
A little girl, who,
is now a good thief too!

John Doriot has wanted to be a writer since he was in the second grade and is fulfilling a dream every day when he sits down to write. He has published 12 books to date. Two of his books, *Litter* and *Grimmer Folk Tales*, were recipients of the Georgia Independent Author of the Year Awards in 2022, for best Horror/Thriller and best collection of short stories.

John was born in Roanoke, Virginia, and grew up in Bristol, Tennessee. A graduate of the University of Tennessee, he has lived in Augusta, Georgia for 32 years, where he retired after a long career in healthcare. He has been married for 43 years and has one son, one granddaughter, and a dog, Oreo. When he is not writing, he loves working in his garden or traveling with his wife and dog, especially to visit their granddaughter. If he is not doing any of the above activities, you will find him reading or searching for the next great book to read!

www.ingramcontent.com/pod-product-compliance
Lightning Source LLC
Chambersburg PA
CBHW030303130626
46549CB00002B/671